Plants, ANIMALS, and Humid Beans

Fun tales from NEA members

edited by
Leona Hiraoka

NEA PROFESSIONAL LIBRARY
National Education Association
Washington, D.C.

Copyright © 1997 by National Education Association of the United States
Cartoons: Copyright © 1997 by George Abbott, Donna Barstow,
Martha Campbell, Dave Carpenter, David Harbaugh
First Printing: September 1997

Editor: Leona Hiraoka
Graphic Designer: Bruce Steinke / Brushwood Thicket Productions
Illustrator, cover and chapters: Krystle Ashley Gosine, age 9
Production Coordinator: Ann Marie Bohan
Editorial Assistants: Danilo Lunaria, Alice Trued, Vernice Woodland

Special thanks to: Marsha Blackburn, Kristine Alvarez, Tammy Reiss

Printed in the United States of America
ISBN 0-8106-1880-X

10 9 8 7 6 5 4 3 2 1

Library of Congress Cataloging-in-Publication Data
Plants, animals, and humid beans: fun tales from NEA members
edited by Leona Hiraoka.
p.   cm.
ISBN 0-8106-1880-X (pbk.)
1. Teachers—United States—Miscellanea.
2. Teachers—United States—Humor.
3. National Education Association of the United States.
I. Hiraoka, Leona, 1962-
II. National Education Association of the United States
LB1775.2.P486   1997   97–33434
371.1'002'07—dc21   CIP

recycled paper

Table of Contents

CHAPTER 1
School Day Smiles

In my third grade music class, a student came to me and said that he didn't like Mozart very much. I asked why, and he replied, "I tried calling Mozart on the telephone last night and he never answered."

When I explained to him that Mozart had been dead for 200 years, the student answered, "Then why did you write his phone number on the wall?"

I looked at the wall and saw a poster I'd made, which read:

Wolfgang Amadeus Mozart
1756-1791

Michael Fridgen
Pine City, Minnesota

As I introduced Munro Leaf's classic book *The Story of Ferdinand* to my first and second grade class, I told the students how I'd loved this book as a child and how happy it made me to be able to share it with them.

I read the story out loud and displayed the book's pen-and-ink drawings. When we were through, I waited for the class's reaction.

"Well," said one little boy judiciously, "that was before they had color!"

Julie Drew
Evanston, Illinois

One day, while I had playground duty at our middle school, the principal came outside. One of the students approached him and told him of a problem she was having with some boys.

He told her to just ignore them and they would stop bothering her. He added that he knew this answer because "I have a minor in psychology in college."

The principal then asked the student if she knew what that meant. She nodded, looked at her feet, and said quietly, "Yes—that means you weren't very good at it."

Annette Davis
Canton, Ohio

Our school principal keeps a "goody box" in her office to encourage students to share their accomplishments with her.

I recently sent my kindergarten students to her with a list of basic sight words they could read independently. As they came back with their selections from her treat box, I asked one little guy, "Did you read the words for her?"

He replied, with the innocence of a five-year-old, "She could already read them!"

Denise Blandford
Cottageville, West Virginia

In my fourth grade math class, I explained that the symbols "<" and ">" mean, respectively, "less than" and "more than." Then, after giving several examples at the blackboard, I asked the class if anyone could explain what the symbols represented.

"That's easy," replied one eager volunteer. "The sign on the left means rewind, and the one on the right means fast forward."

Robert Papp
Peotone, Illinois

I began my seventh year of teaching by moving down to the first grade. On my first day there, a very earnest six-year-old asked me in the first hour if I was going to teach them to read. I smiled and said, yes, I would.

After lunch she repeated her question,

and I reassured her. As I dismissed the class at the end of the day, this sweet little child burst into tears. I asked what was wrong, and she wailed, "You forgot to teach us to read!"

That was my wake-up call to the difference in time frame from upper elementary to primary.

Annette Karrer
Ridgecrest, California

As my first graders were washing their hands for lunch, I overheard one boy say the word "sex." I had no idea in what context he used it, but there was an audible gasp from his classmates.

Deciding to take the teachable moment, I turned to my students and asked, "Did you just gasp because Willy said the word 'sex'?"

Now their eyes were as big as saucers.

"Sex is not a bad word," I continued. "In fact, we have two sexes in this room—the male sex and the female sex."

Then Rachel piped up with, "And insects!"

Laurie Freeburg
Ames, Iowa

"Wow! If we learn from our mistakes, I ought to be a genius by now."

When I tried to contact a seventh grader's parents by phone a while back, I found only a younger sibling at home.

"Can I leave a message?" I asked.

"No," he replied. "We don't have an answering machine."

Claudia Woolverton
Talihina, Oklahoma

When I taught third grade in Philadelphia, our fall field trip included a visit to Independence Hall. Before the excursion, I talked about the famous site and its history, trying to place people and events in perspective. I felt confident my students were prepared as we walked through the historic building.

After my class completed the guided tour, the ranger asked if anyone had any questions. He'd just finished pointing out which famous Americans sat at which desks when one student queried, "Where did John F. Kennedy sit?"

So much for prior knowledge.

Carol Fischer
Lake Barrington, Illinois

February 1960 had been an exciting and challenging first month of teaching for me, fresh out of college at the age of 21. Keeping a fifth/sixth grade split class running proved to be dizzying but rewarding work.

Our very old-fashioned principal had the quaint tradition of delivering our paychecks to us in the classroom. The students and I were immersed in various projects when she arrived with my first payment, so she quietly placed the envelope in my hand and left.

One alert student noticed this and

asked, "What was that?"

"My paycheck," I replied.

"Oh," said the student, "I didn't know you worked!"

Kathleen Juntunen
Bloomfield Hills, Michigan

Even 20-odd years ago, when teaching basic grammar involved old-fashioned drills and practice exercises, I never felt very successful going over and over the textbook's rules. But I was young and determined to do it the "accepted" way. I spent a week hammering away at verb tenses with my eleventh grade English remediation class.

Finally I felt brave enough to give my students a typical "choose the correct verb" test.

Imagine my amazement when one of my most frustrated students scored 96 on his test! Expressing my delight as I returned the test papers, I asked Gary if he'd done some extra studying for the test.

He just shrugged his shoulders and said very matter-of-factly, "No, ma'am. I just seen the word I always say ... and circled the other one."

Judy Jones
Weaverville, North Carolina

In my home economics course, one unit in my foods lab requires that students prepare a starch salad.

One group decided to prepare a macaroni salad from a recipe I'd given them. When evaluating their final product, I asked how they'd changed the recipe, for it didn't taste right.

The students assured me they followed the recipe exactly. It called for "4 cups of cooked macaroni." And to remind them how much macaroni swells compared with other pastas, I'd written in parentheses, "(2 cups uncooked.)"

Turns out they used four cups cooked and two cups uncooked macaroni, which gave their salad a questionable crunchiness.

They provided a good lesson, one that I tell every year when groups select their starch salad recipe.

Doris Oitzman
Victorville, California

I coached football with another coach who had a great sense of humor. We took a lot of our football trips on a regular yellow school bus. Sometimes, on longer trips, we took a Greyhound bus.

Once one of our players asked this coach if we were going to a particular city on a Greyhound.

"Naw," he replied, "we're going on the 'yellow dog.'"

Wallace Dillard
Columbia, Tennessee

"I can't get into school ever since they installed the metal detector."

One Monday morning, as my first graders were working on a map lesson, I announced, "Today we are going to learn about the capital of Illinois. Does anyone already know the capital of Illinois?"

A lone, eager hand shot up from the second table, waving frantically. I acknowledged the owner of the enthusiastic wave. And very calmly and confidently the young geographer answered, "The capital of Illinois is ... the letter 'I'!" (Another moment convincing me that first grade is the greatest!)

Jo Fryer
Long Grove, Illinois

During recess one day, two first graders were throwing stones. Taking them aside to explain the dangers of their actions, I asked, "Jessica, did you throw stones at Robert?"

"No," she replied precociously, "I missed him every time."

Ada Olsen
Bridgewater, Massachusetts

Near the end of an exhausting day of teaching art classes, I suggested to one of the fourth grade boys that he bring in some items from home for his sculpture. He said that he couldn't do that because his mom worked and there wouldn't be time to gather such things.

Because I was tired and also had young children at home, I sympathized and said, "I know how your mom feels."

He glanced up at me and said, "Oh! Do you work somewhere?"

Jan Smolik
Alma, Nebraska

I teach in an alternative learning program for 12- to 15-year-olds. Last year, I was correcting a student's science workbook. It was a hard chapter, and he was getting all the answers right. Because he'd never asked for help, I suspected that perhaps he'd gotten the book's answer key somehow.

My suspicions were confirmed when I got to the last page of the chapter. The final five questions were answered, "Answers may vary."

Margo McKay
Hutchinson, Minnesota

Returning from lunch, I was greeted by Erika waving the fortune from her noon time fortune cookie. "Mrs. Medina, read my fortune!" she shouted.

"You will make a name for yourself," I read.

Quickly, she grabbed it from me, held it in the air, and joyously proclaimed, "Kimberly!"

Jane Medina
Orange, California

In Berks County, Pennsylvania, we are proud of our farm families and their contributions to our society. We select a "Dairy Princess"—a high school student— to visit classes and educate students about dairy production and farm life.

On the day of the visit to my class, my kindergartners were excited about meeting a real princess. When she arrived and was introduced, one of my kids took a look at her chaperone and blurted out, "That must be the Dairy Queen!"

Patsy Sabold
Wyomissing Hills, Pennsylvania

On a high school selection form, my eighth graders were asked, "Whom do you live with?" One student wrote her father's name.

The next line on the form said, "Relationship."

The girl wrote, "Good."

Tammy Luebke
Milwaukee, Wisconsin

In my sixth grade exploratory foreign language class, we were doing a comparison chart of family words in several languages. From the chart, students would create a family portrait.

One girl volunteered the word "jerk" in Italian. "I think we should include this word on our chart," she noted, "because some families might have jerks in them."

Jewell Kern
Wheeling, Illinois

When we received a surprise visit from our superintendent of schools, instead of using conventional introductions, I asked the students in my sixth grade class if they knew who our gentleman visitor was.

Several students raised their hand, but I noticed one boy in particular, grinning from ear to ear and waving his hand.

"Gary," I asked, "would you like to tell the class our visitor's name?"

He laid his hand on the desk, looked confidently at me, and exclaimed, "That's Boris Yeltsin!"

Some of the kids snickered, and Gary had a look of total disbelief on his face. We'd been studying about Russia's leaders, and he noticed the resemblance.

After a moment, I regained my composure and explained to the rest of the class that Gary was correct in one sense—although the gentleman was not Mr. Yeltsin, he was indeed a great leader.

Everyone seemed satisfied, Gary's confidence was restored (and his grin returned), and I then made the formal introductions.

Sandy Fralin
Clayton, North Carolina

A first grader came into my art room one day and noticed the poster of the painting *The Starry Night* by Vincent Van Gogh.

"Wow," he said. "Who made that picture?"

"Vincent Van Gogh," I replied.

He looked at it thoughtfully for a few minutes and said, "That's really good. He must be in the *second* grade."

Diane Balsley
Oak Creek, Wisconsin

"I can't believe it.
Even my fever is low grade!"

21

I recently praised one of my "little" kindergartners by saying, "Wow, you are so smart!"

He simply responded, "I don't want to be smarter—just bigger."

Susan West
Fremont, California

In our school building, some of the teachers volunteer to run the office at noon so that the secretaries can have a work-free lunch period.

One day at noon, one of my students wanted to call her mother. I told her to ask the office people if she could use the phone. She returned in a very short time, so I asked if she'd made the call.

"No," she replied, "I didn't ask. There were just teachers in there, no people."

Judy Smith
Milton, Vermont

Last year, when I taught a first/second split grade, I encouraged my students to ask each other for help with reading assignments.

First grader Ruven was reading and came across the sentence, "¿Dónde está Luis?" (Where is Luis?) He turned to Marisol, pointed to the first word, and asked, "¿Qué es esta palabra?" (What is this word?)

Marisol answered, "Dónde." (Where.)

Puzzled, Ruven again pointed to the word and asked, "¿Qué es esta palabra?"

Marisol again replied, "Dónde."

"Aquí," Ruven shouted, pointing to the word.

Marisol again answered, "Dónde."

Finally Ruven, frustrated and angry, came to me and said, "¡Marisol no quiere ayudarme!" (Marisol doesn't want to help me!)

Rick Tyler
North Hollywood, California

While teaching singular and plural nouns in fifth grade spelling, I asked Alvin to give me the plural form of the word "mosquito." He had trouble, so I prodded him by asking, "If one *mosquito* bites you, you'd say, 'A mosquito bit me.' So what would you say if two of them bit you?"

He replied, "I'd say ouch!"

Quinsola Elliott
Biloxi, Mississippi

On the elementary report card used in my school district, student progress is evaluated on a scale of 1-4. Skill areas that are not being evaluated for a marking period are designated with a slash (/).

After looking over his report card, one of my first graders proudly informed his parents that he'd received 23 threes, 43 fours—and a few spares.

Patricia Kuxhaus
Northville, Michigan

On their first library visit for the new school year, a first grade class was lined up waiting to check out books. Then I overheard one boy say to another, "This is just like the old days in kinder-garten."

David Keyes
Salt Lake City, Utah

To give my fourth graders an opportu-nity to tell me what they'd like me to do differently, I asked them to write a jour-nal entry on the topic "If I Were the Teacher."

Jason surprised me with his response: "If I were the teacher, I would quit and get a new job. I would be a fisherman and catch crabs."

Gloria Weaver
Alpena, Michigan

Mrs. Ancell's bilingual second grade class had physical education last period with me. As part of the lesson closure, I told the students that they would be dismissed if someone could answer my next question. With all eyes fixed on me, I asked, "Who can tell me the capital of Nevada?"

A half-dozen hands shot in the air and eagerly began waving. I called upon Xylina, who quickly stood up and confidently answered, "N!"

Randy Gronert
Las Vegas, Nevada

During my first grade physical education class, a little girl had a baby tooth fall out on the floor.

Since she couldn't tell me where she lost the tooth, I asked all my students to fan out and search the gym floor, for I knew how important it was for her to find it.

After a minute or so of searching, a little boy in the far corner of the gym yelled, "What color was it?"

Steve Bilikam
Powell, Ohio

Prior to administering an informal reading assessment to an incoming first grader, I asked, "Josh, when is your birthday?"

"August," he replied.

There was a pause as I watched his eyes grow wide. Josh looked at me in astonishment and exclaimed, "*All* my birthdays are in August!"

Catherine Dart
Dunstable, Massachusetts

I am a Title 1/Reading Recovery teacher—and recently I was named Teacher of the Year at my elementary school.

One of my former students saw me in the hall the day following the announcement.

"Miss Miller," he exclaimed, "I hear you're finally a teacher!"

Pam Miller
Kirkwood, Missouri

CHAPTER 2
Could You Spell That?

During Halloween, I had two first grade boys complete an unfinished drawing of a cat. When they were done, I asked one of them to show me the cat's paw.

He looked intently at the picture but made no reply.

Again, I asked, "Where's the cat's paw?"

After being asked a third time, the boy finally replied, "I reckon he's at work."

Denise Davis
Rural Retreat, Virginia

As I distributed a quiz to my seventh grade English class, one student asked how they should prepare the paper's heading. I responded, "Write your name, and then wait."

After a few seconds, I heard a shy girl's voice from the back of the room ask, "Well, I can understand why you want us to write our names on the paper, but why would you want to know our weight?"

As soon as she realized what I'd meant, no one giggled more about this incident than the girl who asked the question.

Robert Ritzer
Ramsey, New Jersey

A t the beginning of first grade, we assess students who might be eligible to receive Title I Reading help. One part of the assessment involves having them write all the words they know how to spell. Usually, after writing their name and maybe a couple of more words, they are stumped. So we prompt them.

One little girl wrote "cat," so I asked her if she could spell "dog."

"Sure," she said with a big smile. "B-I-N-G-O."

Pat Manor
Howell, Michigan

When my kindergartners were reading different versions of the story *The Mitten*, a parent volunteer approached me and told me her daughter said we were talking about "virgins" in class!

The surprised parent tried to get more information from her daughter. "You know, mom," she was told, "like there is a Disney Cinderella, and another Cinderella. Different virgins!"

Ah, the parent figured out, her daughter meant "versions"—and we both had a good laugh!

Laura Hoyler
Ashburn, Virginia

I live in a primarily agricultural area. During a class discussion about community workers, one of my kindergarten students asked what kind of job Mr. Delaney had.

"He's a pharmacist," I replied.

"Oh," said the student. "What kind of farmer is that?"

Karen Delaney
Fullerton, Nebraska

**"This is an *aptitude* test, William.
We already know you have an *attitude*!"**

At the end of the year, teachers at our building are required to inventory rooms and fill out a variety of forms. At the last teachers meeting, we received a packet of our forms and a checklist of other items to turn in to the principal before we left for the summer.

The beginning of the list read: "Orders for next year, Money deposits, Attendance cards, and Uncleared *lust*."

It should have read "Uncleared *list*," of course. But we got quite a laugh out of the thought of turning in our uncleared lust to our principal.

Julie Moffett
Portsmouth, Ohio

During winter vacation, one of my kindergarten English-as-a-second-language students returned to his native Croatia to visit his grandparents. After

New Year's, Igor did not return to school. January and February passed, and still no Igor.

So when he returned to our school in March, several of us teachers surrounded him and showered him with our expressions of joy.

He looked at us impassively until I said, "Oh, Igor, you have grown so tall. You look so grown up." With that, he raised himself to his full height, crossed his arms in front of his chest, and stated, "I have sex!"

After several moments of shocked speechlessness, a memory of a birthday flashed into my consciousness.

"Igor, did you have a birthday in Croatia?" I asked.

"Yes," he beamed. "I no five. I have sex!"

Sarah Bingaman
Elmhurst, Illinois

37

One of my kindergartners boasted to me that she could spell "boy" without even looking. She then closed her eyes and proceeded, "B ... zero ... Y."

Barbara Reed
Tracy, California

While I was substituting in a fifth grade class, confusion began immediately after I administered a spelling test.

One boy said, "Our teacher doesn't give us 21 words." Another student spoke up and said she only had 20 words. Then another said she had 21.

So I asked for a show of hands to find out how many words I had dictated. To my surprise, about 10 students had the 21 words, while the remaining had 20.

I asked to see some of the tests with

21 words. Sure enough—there was an
extra word at #11, and the word was
"QUIET."

Nan Roberge
Mount Vernon, New Hampshire

**"When you stir the soup, might we
say that you're groping for words?"**

A short video that I showed my junior level college prep class noted that Henry Wadsworth Longfellow's second wife died when her light summer dress caught fire after hot sealing wax dripped on it.

When the clip ended, one of my students asked, "That was an awful way to die—but why did they have hot wax on the ceiling?"

Brenda Abbott
Bailey, Colorado

I thought my tenth grade special education global studies class had a good grasp on the presented material until a glossary test on the rise of czarist Russia revealed the following answers:

- serf: on big waves
- feudalism: I knock you out
- Russification: Russian knock

- Romanov Dynasty: eat dinner at Romanov's

Fortunately, these test answers were an exception, and the rest of the class did indeed understand the lesson.

Lynn Stankowitz
North Babylon, New York

One day, while I had the dreaded cafeteria duty, David became upset that someone had taken his pencil. I restated his concern about the theft. He then told me that he wasn't as upset about the pencil as he was about the fact that the thief wouldn't own up to his misdeed.

"So it's not that he took your pencil," I said. "It's the principle of the whole thing."

"No," said David. "The principal had nothing to do with it."

Ginny Gelbach
Littleton, Colorado

CHAPTER 3
By Definition

Just before spring vacation, I announced to my high school geometry students that they would have a big review assignment to do over the break.

"What kind of a dictionary do teachers have?" asked one of my students. "Don't they know what 'break' means?"

"They don't have a regular dictionary," answered another student. "They use the teachers' edition."

Lawrence Orloff
San Francisco, California

After completing a lesson on library procedure that included distinguishing fiction from non-fiction, I assigned my fifth grade students their first book report of the year. They were to report on any non-fiction hero of their choice.

As the class filtered through the school library in search of books on their heroes,

I noticed Jared, a freckle-faced redhead, frantically perusing the card catalog. A few minutes later, he dejectedly shuffled over to me lamenting, "Mr. Chaney, I can't find any books on my hero, Superman."

Just as I was about to inform him that Superman was a fictitious character, his classmate Angie blurted out haughtily, "Of course you can't find anything on Superman, silly. That's a fiction name. You need to look under Clark Kent."

Jerome "Jody" Chaney
Pittsburg, California

As I worked at my computer, a kinder-garten girl popped in and asked, "Whatcha doing?"

"Typing a letter," I replied.

"Oh," she said, "is it 'A'?"

Michael Nichols
Jackson County, North Carolina

When I first started teaching, I had a remedial class in biology. We spent a long time learning about the plant and animal kingdom, and, of course, we studied the human body.

On a test, I asked the students to name the kinds of life on Earth. One little girl wrote, "Plants, Animals, and Humid Beans."

Douglas Dietrich
Tucson, Arizona

After researching election issues earlier this school year, one of my language arts students reported on a lobbyist taking "potshots" at Congress.

Then he assured me that he'd never use drugs—because he wouldn't ever want to take pot shots in the future!

Carol Fredrikson
Two Rivers, Wisconsin

It was almost Election Day, and I decided to give my kindergarten class a lesson on voting. We had a pumpkin in our room, so I decided that we would "vote" on whether our jack-o-lantern would have a funny or a scary face by raising hands.

Then we discussed the upcoming election and the problems parents would have if everyone had to raise their hand to vote.

I explained that grown-ups go to a special place to vote, a place where everyone votes and the votes are easily counted. And I was very proud of myself for teaching such a complicated topic to a group of four- to five-year-olds.

As we were cleaning up, one little girl told me that she'd gone with her grandpa to vote. I asked her to tell the class about it. So she explained to everyone that they went to a place called OTB (off-track betting) and her grandpa voted for a horse—but it didn't win!

Sandy Davis
Hamden, Connecticut

Michael stood by my desk, waiting for me to grade his math test. He studied the calendar on the bulletin board for a while, then asked excitedly, "Hey, are we getting a new moon?"

Beth Panitz
Millersville, Maryland

A few days after a new student had joined my class, I received a message from her mom asking for a list of supplies that the student would be needing.

At the end of the day, I sat down with the student to go over the supply list. I asked her if she had crayons, and she said yes. Then I asked if she had Magic Markers.

She looked at me strangely for a moment and said, "Well, I have markers, but they're not magic."

Carol Nanney
McKenzie, Tennessee

"I want to get something straight. Am I the opposite sex or is she?"

While I was giving a national standard-
ized test to my first graders, one of
the very bright boys raised his hand for
help. I went over and saw he was stuck on
the definition of the word "cellar."

He whispered to me that the correct
answer was not there—adding that "a
place to keep wine" was not one of the
choices.

Only in California!

Jackie Panigada
Fontana, California

During a language arts lesson, a first-
grade student of Asian descent presented me with her completed list of
compound words.

I noticed that she'd incorrectly included
"putting" on her list and advised her that
this was not a compound.

She insisted that it was, so I asked,

"What two words do you see in 'putting'?"

"'Put' and 'ting,'" she replied.

"'Ting' is not a word," I said.

"Yes, it is," she insisted. "It's my father's name!"

Maryanne Mead
Bridgewater, New Jersey

It was picture day for my kindergartners, and envelopes had been sent home a few days earlier so parents could enclose their payment. On picture day, I received a call from a parent informing me that her child's money was in the zippered compartment of his backpack.

When it came time to collect the money, I reminded this student that his mother said to check his backpack. He came back and told me that there wasn't any money.

I told him to look again, and this time

he came back and said, "No, there's no money—only a check."

Louise Murray
Braintree, Massachusetts

After displaying 12 new vocabulary words on flashcards, I asked my second grade students to supply the correct word for the sentence, "You turn a _____ to open a door."

Being exposed to English slang through his older siblings, one confident little boy raised his hand and boldly announced, "Doork-nob!"

Dianne Kintzer
Reading, Pennsylvania

While helping a fourth grade class use the library, I was approached by one child who whispered that the cluster of boys around the large dictionary was looking up a "dirty word."

Intrigued, I casually strolled over and asked what they were trying to find. One young man, very red-faced, confessed in an ashamed tone that it was ... "bra."

Nancy Nash
Gladwin, Michigan

"My friend Edward is bilingual.
He can talk to boys and girls."

Several years ago, one of my freshman girls decided to call up a tenth grade boy just to talk. When the young man's mother answered, the young lady asked to speak to Bob.

"Junior or senior?" asked the boy's mother.

"Uh," stammered the young lady, "I think he's a sophomore."

Dennis Flynn
Norristown, Pennsylvania

I assigned my first-period civics class ten vocabulary words and asked the students to not only define them, but to write a short story using each term so I could check comprehension.

Shawn obviously didn't comprehend the terms "political party" or "two-party system," but at least he made me smile.

"Every month, Bob would throw a wild

'political party,'" wrote Shawn. "He would serve sodas, chips, and dip. Sometimes he believed in the 'two-party system.' That's when he'd have two parties in one month!"

Al Sturgeon
Paragould, Arkansas

During reading time, I discussed the word "forefront" with my fifth graders. After a definition and a couple of sentences using the word, I asked Willie to give us his sentence using the word.

Willie obviously wasn't paying close attention. Yet after bringing his gaze down off the ceiling, he looked at me and replied, "My baby brother has four front teeth."

Randell Snipes
Memphis, Tennessee

O ur class was studying the growth and development of cities. While studying Detroit, we took a closer look at the automobile industry and discussed the importance of the assembly line.

At the conclusion of the unit, a test was given. One item read, "Explain how an assembly line works."

A very clever third grade boy responded, "It works like a charm."

He, of course, received credit for his answer.

Vanessa DeCapite
Euclid, Ohio

E ach spring, my second grade class plans a field trip to a museum and art gallery. While discussing our plans, I told the class about the souvenir shop at the museum, saying that they could bring souvenir money to buy something.

One little boy replied, "We don't have any of that souvenir money at our house. Can I bring real money instead?"

Carla Plager
Table Rock, Nebraska

I recently held a school-wide election for our middle/high school. The parties represented were Democrat, Republican, Reform, and Libertarian. I thought the students responded very well, and many of them seemed quite interested in the election process.

A few days later, a middle school student informed me that he had a question. He wanted to know how the librarian on the ballot did in the election.

Beth Bohnert
Petersburg, Indiana

You can never take for granted what terms students are familiar with.

In our seventh grade geography class, my students came across a paragraph that discussed "Caucasians." I assumed everyone knew what a Caucasian was—until one student raised his hand during our discussion and asked for a definition.

One by one, students came forward with these definitions:

- That hot, spicy food in Louisiana. (Cajun)
- When you mix all kinds of stuff together, you get a Caucasian. (Concoction)
- When you get hit on the head, you'll end up getting a Caucasian. (Concussion)

William Aleksiewicz
Cochranton, Pennsylvania

I n our school, quite a few students speak English as a second language. In compiling my yearly report, I have to survey the new students.

I strive to phrase the questions in a way that won't confuse them. So I asked one kindergartner, "When you first started talking, what language did you use?"

She gazed at me seriously and said, "Baby talk."

Barbara Moody-Hamilton
Memphis, Tennessee

My students were assigned to write a sentence using their new vocabulary words. For the word "hinge," one student wrote, "I went to the biggest hinge in town."

The definition that I'd given them? "Hinge: a swinging joint."

Carol Hoover
Norcross, Georgia

In an early draft of his book report on *Of Mice and Men*, one student in my freshman English class characterized Curley as "cocky and arrogant." I circled the statement and wrote in the margin, "Redundant"—a term he should have been familiar with from usage in class.

When I saw this student's final revision, I had to laugh. He'd changed his statement to read that Curley was "cocky and redundant."

Karen White
Columbia, Illinois

CHAPTER 4

Animal Attractions

It was a very cold winter morning, and my third graders were busy completing a writing assignment. I was at the computer center writing a newsletter when I felt a cold draft on my back.

Without turning around, I said, "Would someone close the door, please. There's a draft coming down the hallway."

Suddenly every student rushed from their seat, raced to the door, and looked down the hallway expectantly. I was flabbergasted and said, "What are you doing?"

To which they all exclaimed, "We want to see the giraffe!"

Betty Strawcutter
Sylvania, Ohio

I overheard a colleague and a student discussing a reading passage comparing the woolly mammoth with elephants. My colleague asked the student why he thought woolly mammoths had so much more hair than modern-day elephants.

The student thought for a while and then replied, "I guess long hair must have been in style back then."

Sandra Schwartz
South Windsor, Connecticut

When I was an elementary librarian, I tried to expose my students to non-fiction books in an attempt to awaken all those hidden interests.

One day, a third grader approached me with a cookbook titled *The Pet's Cookbook*, full of recipes for dogfood, catfood, and various pet treats.

"Ah," I thought, "a budding cook."

"Mrs. Shaw," the student asked, "why would anyone want to cook their pet?"

Janet Shaw
Newark, Delaware

Many years ago, while I was teaching junior high, my family bought a small farm to gain the experience of raising horses. When my students heard about this, they wanted to come out and ride, which they did frequently.

One day, I announced that there would be no riding today, because the horses were to be shod—a word that apparently wasn't familiar to them. Immediately there was a look of horror and bewilderment on their faces, as they wondered why I would have to shoot my horses.

Frank Mazurek
Ithaca, New York

I had just arrived at the first grade room to teach art when a little girl raised her hand. When I called on her, she said, "My cat just had kittens. Do you know why?"

"No," I said. "Why?"

She came up to me and whispered, "Because she has a husband."

Jeanne LaPlante
Merrillan, Wisconsin

My fifth graders were working at the chalkboard to find the perimeters of rectangles with only one length and one width marked. Seeing that one young lady was having difficulty, I went over to help. She'd added only the two sides that were marked.

I suggested that if the rectangle were a fence, her dog would be gone. She stared at the drawing and began thinking very hard. I asked what she was thinking, so I could lead her in the right direction.

She replied, "I'm trying to figure out how to get my dog back."

Nina Garofalo
St. Louis, Missouri

'm a pre-K teacher aide, and during circle time I was showing students pictures of all sorts of animals. As I held the pictures up, the children would call out what the animal is—a monkey, a bear, an elephant, etc.

When I came to a picture of a seal, I held it up and said, "Oh boy, that's a tuffy."

To which the whole class replied, "IT'S A TUFFY!"

Roberta Sclafani
Hollywood, Florida

One of my kindergarten students brought in a bird nest for show and tell. When asked if the nest had any eggs in it when he found it, the boy answered no.

The class began thinking of reasons why the nest had been found empty— "Maybe the eggs already hatched," "Maybe they fell out of the nest and cracked."

Then the boy who'd brought in the nest suggested, "Maybe the birds weren't married."

Margaret Palmieri
Columbia, Maryland

69

As a follow-up activity to a literature section about zoo animals, my kindergarten class was making a menu featuring items the animals might like.

As I observed their work, Corey confidently reported, "My grandmother feeds the lions."

Surprised that a lion might be found in our small, rural community in southern Pennsylvania, I asked, "Here in Breezewood?"

"Sure," he answered, "at the fire hall each month."

Miriam Peck
Everett, Pennsylvania

My class of first graders had enjoyed many Curious George books. We all envied the Man with the Big Yellow Hat— wouldn't it be fun to have a pet like George!

Somehow we'd never read the first book, where the Man meets George. Finally, one day a little girl brought that book in for me to read.

I had just reached the part where the Man tricks George with his hat when one of my boys, with a look of pure horror on his face, yelled out, "The Man with the Big Yellow Hat is a poacher!"

At least he set the stage for conversations on animal rights and how times have changed since George's birth.

Catherine Buotte
Bath, Maine

A s I was checking off my first graders' homework, I noticed that Jose hadn't turned in his homework envelope. I asked him if he'd done his homework, and he responded by telling me that he did, but that his dog had eaten it. Since I'd heard that excuse a million times, I just figured he didn't do it.

Jose went back to his backpack to get his folder and returned with a somewhat guilt-ridden look on his face. As I took his homework papers out, I noticed that they were damp, wrinkled, and full of teeth marks!

The dog really *did* eat his homework.

I was still able to read it, and Jose got the credit.

Karen Amberly Joe
Moreno Valley, California

One day, I was telling students in my second grade ESL class that I was tired and yawning because the neighbor's dog had barked all night. Then we all practiced yawning and barking.

The discussion then moved on to other night sounds: cats fighting, police sirens, dripping faucets. One very serious child then said that the lions keep him awake. So we practiced roaring.

Then I, in my misguided sense that adults know everything, told him that he probably heard cars going by. He was determined that they were lions.

When this student's family picked him up after school, I mentioned the conversation about lions. And his father said yes, the lions did keep them awake—they lived next door to Milinda, first lady of magic, and her lions, camels, etc.

Only in Las Vegas!

Karon Lee
Las Vegas, Nevada

CHAPTER 5
Personal Parts

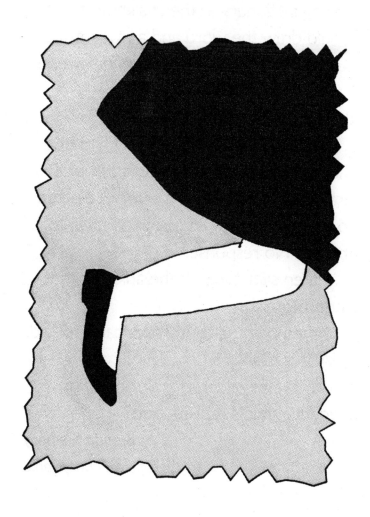

I was working on the plural forms of words ending in "f" and "fe" with my group of special ed fifth graders. We were playing pictionary at the chalkboard—I would draw the word and a student would come up and spell it. If I drew one knife, they'd write "knife." If I drew two, they'd write "knives."

Time was running out, and I had one more word: calf. Rather than attempt a drawing of a young farm animal, I elected to draw a leg with an arrow pointing to the calf. No response.

I then said it wasn't the ankle or the knee. Nothing.

I then pointed to my own calf and said, "What is *this*?"

With a bewildered look, one of my students timidly replied, "Fat?"

Brenda Kennedy
Clearfield, Pennsylvania

I was teaching my first graders about President's Day a few years ago. I'm African American, and as I was closing my lesson on the topic, I said, "Now remember, boys and girls, President Lincoln freed people like me."

A certain little boy went home and told his mother about the lesson. And she couldn't wait to come and tell me that she was very happy to learn that "Lincoln freed women."

It's nice to know that children don't see color.

Donna Hill
Amarillo, Texas

As a reading specialist, I frequently visit the second and third grade classrooms. My young students are amused by my name. They often call me "Mr. Moose" or even "Mr. Goose."

Last year, a sad-faced second grader with a stomachache appeared in the health suite.

"Which teacher sent you here?" asked Nurse Collins.

"Dr. Seuss," he replied.

"Dr. Seuss?" she said. "I didn't know he worked here."

"You know," the child said, "that old teacher who helps us kids learn to read."

I think it is quite an honor to be mistaken for the beloved author of children's stories.

Daniel Loose
Leesport, Pennsylvania

As I was teaching my sixth grade art class about the artist Frida Kahlo, I mentioned that she was born in 1907 and died in 1954. She died, I noted, at the age of 47.

As I went on to recount some of the interesting things that happened in her life, a student's hand shot up. When I called on him, he asked, "Did Frida Kahlo die of old age?"

Shocked, I replied, "I hope not!"

Charlene Armstrong
Galesburg, Illinois

"I said, 'How long were you a band instructor?' "

During his bus ride home, my nephew Danny, a second grader, saw his street go by and started to yell, "You passed my street."

The bus monitor informed him that he was on the wrong bus and, after dropping off all the other students, took Danny back to school. There his principal and his mother were waiting for him.

"Danny, didn't you notice these weren't the regular kids on your bus?" asked the principal.

"You know, come to think of it," Danny replied, "I was wondering why everyone was on the wrong bus."

Vinny Carbone
Monroe, Connecticut

After a hard day in middle school, I received this note on my desk:

"If you ever want to see your file cabinet key again, go to the commons area at midday and bring the peanut butter cups. Sincerely, Hungry and Desperate."

Laurie Garcia
Pueblo West, Colorado

D. Barstow

**"If we run into one of my students,
I'll have to stop being normal
and act like a teacher for a minute."**

Due to my father's illness, I missed the first week of school with my third graders.

In January, we were reading *The Titanic*, and I told the class that my great-uncle had died on that ship.

One little boy looked up at me and said, "Boy, you're having a bad year. First your dad gets sick, and now your great-uncle dies on the *Titanic*!"

Suzanne Howe
Dodgeville, Wisconsin

Though I am a recently retired teacher, I continue to do some substitute teaching in my community. One day, I was early for my meeting with a fifth grade class, so I walked into the cafeteria. There two first grade chaps were having a good old time, and when they spotted me, they asked who I was.

I joked that I was the boss. They quickly responded that this couldn't be, since their principal was the boss at the school. So I said I was the boss of the whole world.

As I stepped back out to meet my class, I overheard one of the boys whisper seriously to the other, "I think he's God!"

Bill Reinert
Two Rivers, Wisconsin

My fifth grade learning center students were all diligently working on their homework projects. One of the boys was struggling with the composition of an interview (of me!) that he'd conducted earlier in the week. All of sudden he blurted out, "Mrs. West, where were you born?"

Quietly, I answered, "Minneapolis, Minnesota."

"Ah, man, how do you spell all of that?" he asked.

"That's a hard one," I said. "I'll write it on the board for you."

After I did, one of the other students watching all of this shouted, "Mrs. West, you were born in *two* places!"

Susan L. West
Dublin, California

My ninth grade health class was full of fun and lively teens. This class always wanted to know my business, including my birthday. In joking with the kids, I gave them a phony date.

Well, several weeks later I was honored at a surprise birthday party. I couldn't have been more shocked—since it wasn't really my birthday. The kids had planned a wonderful dance, decorated a cake, and brought a large assortment of homemade ethnic food.

I will never forget this class and the wonderful memory they created. No, I never told them they had the wrong day.

Joan Forseth
Tacoma, Washington

Last year, on my last day of student teaching in a resource room, I handed out candy bars to the students and thanked them for their attention.

One of the students thanked me in return, and then said, "So, what are you going to be now?"

Cheryl Benson
Sigourney, Iowa

When my daughter was eight, her third grade teacher asked the students what instrument they would like to play.

My daughter wrote, "Flute."

Never having evinced such an interest before, I asked how she came to give this answer.

"Oh," she said, "I couldn't spell 'piano,' so I put 'flute.'"

Jack Sundquist
Tacoma, Washington

My daughter's third grade class was reading about quilt-making in the Old West. So their young first-year teacher brought in a sample quilt. Wanting to impress them with its relevance, she said, "It's right off my bed" as she shook open the quilt.

Out flew a pair of pink underpants— to the delight of dozens of eight-year-olds, who will never forget what a quilt is.

Donna Judd
Fullerton, California

I was a band director from 1948-81. Once, while teaching at a junior high, I took my kindergarten son to see his first symphony concert. After tuning up, the orchestra program began. He was impressed.

After intermission, the tune up began again. My young man nudged me and said, "Dad, they played this song before."

Bill Wilson
Western Springs, Illinois

I t was my first year teaching. All my little second graders were sitting on the carpet. We were discussing different physical characteristics such as hair color and eye color. Now we were moving on to noses.

Being a naive young teacher, I asked, "What do you notice about my nose?" (I have a rather small nose.)

One little girl eagerly raised her hand. I was so glad she was participating and I called on her quickly. She proudly announced, "You have black dots on your nose, Miss Johnson."

Well, that wasn't the response I'd wanted. But I sure learned a lot about phrasing open-ended questions.

Teresa Johnson
Visalia, California

For many years, I served as an elementary school librarian in the Lansing School District. My 1969-70 teaching assignment included both Moores Park and Maple Hill elementary schools.

Unfortunately, early in the school year, I fractured my left cheekbone and needed an operation that required shaving a sizable spot on my head.

The wig I purchased to hide the hair

loss did nothing to enhance my looks. Apprehensive about the reaction of the students, I voiced my concern to the director of school libraries. She, in turn, must have contacted the principals at the two schools.

I don't know what these two gentlemen and their respective staff members said or did, but during the several months that I wore the unbecoming headpiece, not a single child ever commented on or even looked askance at my changed appearance—until the day that I staffed my library post minus the wig.

As I confronted a class of young students at the Maple Hill school, one little girl—still cautious about the "don't mention the wig" taboo—whispered to me, "Oh, Mrs. Pekrul, you've got your own hair back on today. You look so nice again!"

Besides their customary teaching tasks, these wonderful educators had added manners, tactfulness, and compassion.

June (Pekrul) Fahlen
East Lansing, Michigan